Jessie Laidlay Weston

King Arthur and His Knights

A Survey of Arthurian Romance

.

Jessie Laidlay Weston

King Arthur and His Knights
A Survey of Arthurian Romance

ISBN/EAN: 9783337033323

Printed in Europe, USA, Canada, Australia, Japan

Cover: Foto ©Thomas Meinert / pixelio.de

More available books at **www.hansebooks.com**

KING ARTHUR AND HIS KNIGHTS:

A BRIEF INTRODUCTION TO THE STUDY OF ARTHURIAN LITERATURE

KING ARTHUR and his knights! Was there ever a time when to English ears these words were not an "open sesame" to the gates of a Fairy-land, the more charming in that we believed it to be partly, at least, real? Even in the stern Puritan days when romance was a thing to be abhorred of the "saints" Milton could have dreams of devoting an epic to the glory of the British hero. (We wonder what the poet of the *Paradise Lost* would have made of that fascinating and tangled web of Celtic-French fact and fancy!) And yet how little, how very little, we know about them. Let any of us take any twelve of our friends, of those whom we know to be above the average in intelligence and culture, and ask them one by one, what they can tell us of King Arthur, and how we can gain information as to his life and doings, and what shall we be told? Certainly we should be referred to Malory and Tennyson—and there for

A

ten out of the twelve the matter would end. Perhaps, only perhaps, the other two might be able to tell us that there was a history by a certain Geoffrey of Monmouth, out of which a certain Walter Map drew materials to invent the legend of Arthur and the Grail, and it might be, that if exceptionally well informed, our last friend might contradict this statement and say, "No, it was not Map who invented the Grail story at all, but a French poet, called Chrétien."

And, indeed, if we get as much information as that, we shall be fortunate! It is no exaggeration to say the few names just mentioned represent all that is known, and that at second or third hand, by even highly educated people, of this great body of literature. A few years ago a *History of English Poetry* was published, and received with acclamation, in which the writer practically attributed the whole body of Arthurian Romance, so far as he considered it worthy of notice, to Walter Map. Only the other day, in one of our leading journals, there appeared a long article from the pen of a popular writer, who poses as a person of exceptional culture and literary discernment, wherein Wagner's *Parsifal* was severely criticised as a "wide departure from Malory!" So much do even our would-be teachers know of the matter.

There are certainly reasons which might be urged in excuse for this widespread ignorance of a legend which we have every right to claim as national; the greater portion of Arthurian literature is in a foreign tongue, and it is only in comparatively recent years that a systematic attempt has been made to arrive at a clear idea of the date, authorship, and mutual relation of the romances composing the cycle. For long even professed scholars were content with the most meagre, confused, and superficial knowledge on a subject which touches us so nearly.

But have we any right to look on King Arthur as a national hero? It has been objected that since Arthur was a *British* chieftain we are entirely wrong in treating him as an *English* hero. This is surely a pedantic accuracy which over-shoots its own mark; we might as reasonably contend that the French have no right to glory in the *Matière de France*, since Charlemagne was certainly no Frenchman! The truth appears to be that absolute racial identity between hero and hero-worshippers is a factor of minor importance in the case of peoples, who, like the English and the French, are compounded of various racial elements. What *is* essential to a national hero is that he shall have successfully maintained the honour of the *land*. Arthur represented the honour of Britain, Charlemagne that of "*la douce France*," the feeling which glorified both was patriotism in the most exact and accurate sense of the word.

The evolution of Arthur as a national hero, indeed, is a very curious and striking example of the unconquerable vitality and power of impressing itself characteristic of the Celtic genius. We reject, and very reasonably, the tradition which represents the British King as carrying his arms triumphantly through France and Italy, and vanquishing even the power of Rome; but what the *historical* Arthur did not do, the *legendary* Arthur assuredly achieved. Not only did the English people (representative of the Saxon, Danish, and Norman invaders of British soil) take him to their heart, and as they became welded into one folk accept him as the traditionary embodiment of the spirit of their land, but he took captive the imagination alike of France and of Italy. He is immortalised in French verse and in Italian architecture; Sicily claims to be his resting-place; and there is no European literature of any importance which does not contribute its quota to the great mass of Arthurian romance.

Yet a comparatively small proportion only of this literature is in the English tongue. When the Arthurian legend was at the height of its popularity the dominant language was French, and it was in the form of French romance that the *literary* legend became popularised in this land.

Nevertheless it is, I believe, a mistaken view which ascribes this popularity entirely to court influence, and the charm of Chrétien's verse: the legend had not been entirely forgotten in its own land, and re-introduced from without; nor is there any reason to suppose, as some scholars have done, that the knowledge of it was confined exclusively to the survivors of the original inhabitants of the Island. Too much has, I think, been made of the racial animosity existing between Briton and Saxon. We know for instance, that for a period extending over two centuries at least the two nationalities lived side by side in the city of Exeter. Even to-day archæologists will point out where the line of demarcation between the two towns (for such they practically were) ran, nor were the Britons treated as a subjugated folk. William of Malmesbury distinctly says that they enjoyed equal rights with the English. This state of matters lasted well into the tenth century; are we to believe that during all these years the memory of bye-gone strife was kept alive to such an extent that Saxon and Briton never came into friendly contact with each other, held no inter-communion, never inter-married, never made common cause against their common foe the Danes? They ask a great deal who ask us to believe this! Evidence points the other way; in Cornwall, the refuge of the surviving British population we find to-day families bearing a name of such purely *Saxon* origin as Eddy (Æddi) and yet claiming to be of pure

Cornish descent; in East Anglia, a Saxon strong-
hold, we find in the seventh century the British
name of Cadwallon.* Surely it is more reasonable
to suppose that by the transmission of oral legend
the name and fame of the British chief had become
thoroughly familiar to the Saxon population long
before the "literary" stage of evolution had been
reached.

Every folk must have its national hero, and it is
worthy of note that the Saxon or Teutonic heroic
legends never took real root in this land. That
they were introduced we know. Have we not the
poem of *Beowulf?* But Beowulf and his fight
with Grendel and the dragon, were less popular
than the record of how Arthur slew the giant of
Mont S. Michel, and conquered the Demon Cat.
The great *Siegfried* legend certainly came to
these shores, and we find traces of its influence in
Celtic romance; † but the only Teutonic hero who
seems to have gained firm footing on English
ground was *Wieland*, who as *Wayland Smith* still
survives in popular tradition.

On this point see an interesting article by M. Ferd.
Lot in "Romania," No. 109, January 1899. For information regarding the British and Saxon names, &c., I am
indebted to the Rev. Canon Edmonds, Librarian of Exeter
Cathedral.

† *Cf.* Mr. Alfred Nutt's study on the *Mabinogi of Bran-
wen,* "Folk-Lore Record," Vol. V.

Whatever the reasons may have been, the fact remains that as the various nationalities in this island slowly welded themselves into one people, and Briton, Saxon, Dane and Norman became *English*, the hero adopted as their national hero was the chief of the conquered, not of the conquering races. Thus when Geoffrey of Monmouth, drawing upon a work probably compiled by a continental Breton, gave to the world his " *Historia Britonum* " in which the pseudo-historical deeds of Arthur were solemnly related, the book was received with avidity, and Norman and Angevin Kings, without a drop of British blood in their veins, gloried in the renown of their predecessor. His history was bound up with the history of Great Britain, and the inhabitants of that land, recognising this, hailed him as their own.

But, as I said before, in its literary form the Arthurian legend came to us mainly in a foreign tongue. With the scanty materials at our disposal it is difficult to say what was the date, and what the extent, of the original Welsh Arthurian literature. At one time it probably formed a considerable body of romance, but by the twelfth century, from which period the real popularity of the Arthurian legend may be dated, Welsh was, as its very name indicates, an unknown tongue alike to the English-speaking majority of the nation and to the Norman conquerors, and as such had no power of competing with French, the language of the court and the nobility. The survival of the legend as a living force, both here and on the continent, was doubtless due to Celtic influence ; its immense popularity as a Romantic literary cycle was due to French genius.

Thus the main body of Arthurian literature is French, some of the finest poems are German, little, very little is English. Previous to Malory English Arthurian literature consisted of scattered ballads and metrical romances, and these, save for scholars, are practically unreadable. If any student desires to get a clear idea of the slow growth of the English language, and the time it took for the various elements composing it to be welded into a national tongue, I can suggest nothing more illuminating than for him to take three Arthurian romances, say a poem of Chrétien de Troyes with its contemporary German translation, and our *Sir Gawayne and the Grene Knyghte* (the best of our English Arthurian romances) and compare them. If he has any real knowledge of French and German he will not find the two first over-difficult ; there are, of course, obsolete words and obsolete forms of spelling, but read them aloud, and they are quite intelligible. At the close of the twelfth century France and Germany had, each of them, a language and a literature. But the English poem, two centuries later in date and nearer our day than the others, is practically in "an unknown tongue," so little relation does it bear to the modern form of our language. To read it at all is a task which demands great patience—and an excellent glossary!

Previous to the compilation of Sir Thomas Malory, which is almost entirely a translation and abridgment of the later French prose romances, we have no English Arthurian literature accessible, or intelligible, to the general reader. This naturally accounts, in a large measure, for the ignorance of the Arthurian legend common in England; it has also unhappily affected the work of those scholars who have seriously set themselves to study the subject. The *legend* certainly belongs to us, but the *literature* belongs elsewhere, and this fact was at first not sufficiently recognised. Comparatively speaking it is only in our own day that the value of romantic literature has been realised, and its study systematically attempted; for long such subjects were deemed unworthy the attention of a serious scholar. A lifetime might be spent over the elucidation of some obscure Greek or Latin writer (who had, perhaps, left only half a poem behind him), but to attempt to understand the tales in which our forefathers had delighted, on which the childhood of the nation had been fed, was quite beneath the dignity of a learned man. We know better now; we know that if we would understand a folk we must study its tales, and that important evidence of the inter-relation of peoples, the spread of culture from one land to another, the influence of one race on another, is to be gathered from their popular literature. The study of romance means also the study of history, and in the subject we are now considering any student of Arthurian literature will readily admit that historical considerations play no unimportant part.

At first interest in the question naturally shewed itself in printing and making accessible to the public the principal texts. To such writers as Southey, who edited the *Morte d'Arthur;* Ritson, who published several volumes of *Ancient English Metrical Romances;* Dunlop, who wrote a *History of Fiction,* and Sir Frederick Madden, who published a selection of poems dealing with *Sir Gawain,* we owe a debt of gratitude none the less deep because the progress of study has necessitated most of their work being done over again.

Early labourers in this field contented themselves with the reproduction of a MS. Interesting as the work was they hardly held it of sufficient importance to undertake the labour involved in reconstructing the original text by means of careful and critical comparison of all the available MSS. Nor were the materials for such a task at their disposal to the same extent as they are at ours. Much, very much, still remains to be done, but every year facilitates the task; new editions of the various romances are published; critical editions, already in our hands, revised and improved; here and there a search-light is thrown on some special point of interest by means of studies and monographs from the pen of scholars of known repute. But in all this labour it is regretfully to be acknowledged that we, in this land, still lag behind. Of late years the study of romance literature in general and of the Arthurian cycle in particular has made immense strides on the Continent, but any one interested in the matter cannot fail to be struck by the paucity of English works of solid value as compared with the mass of French and German critical literature. To a monograph on the Grail legend, published by a German scholar last year, was appended a list of books dealing with the Arthurian legend; out of two hundred and thirty-six works noted, only *fifteen* bore English names, and of those fifteen not more than seven, at the outside, would be of any solid value for critical purposes.

In a brief study like this it would, of course, be impossible fully to discuss this great body of romance, or to give more than such a sketch of its general character as may serve to guide the reading of any one desirous to make acquaintance, at first hand, with the works of which it is composed. As we shall see, these works are not only many in number but also very diverse in character. We class under the general title of *the Arthurian cycle* a large body of literature, dating for the most part from the latter half of the twelfth and first quarter of the thirteenth centuries, some of which deals only indirectly with the British King. Indeed we are accustomed to include under this heading certain romances, such as the early *Tristan* poems, which have absolutely no connection whatever with Arthur. The fame of the hero-king caused him to become a convenient centre round which to group a circle of recitals of miscellaneous character. Arthur's Court and Arthur's Round Table, had [t]hey ever existed in the form familiar to us, would certainly have drawn to themselves, as to a point of attraction, the most valiant spirits of the land and time; from a literary point of view they operated in precisely the same way—the legend drew to itself and absorbed, more or less completely, other legends, some of older, many of clearly independent origin.

This literature divides itself naturally into two sections, poetry and prose. Which of the two was the earlier has been a much debated question; the view now generally accepted is that the poetical romances preceded the prose. M. Gaston Paris very happily demonstrated this in a study on Chrétien de Troyes' *Chevalier de la Charette*, showing that the poetical version had been transferred, almost literally, to the prose *Lancelot*. It does not, of course, follow that a prose romance was never versified ; for instance, there exists a mediæval Dutch verse rendering of the *Queste*, the only such version known ; here, scholars are unanimously of opinion that the prose contained in all the other MSS. represents the original form.

As a rule the poems, especially the earlier ones, such as the works of Chrétien de Troyes and his German contemporaries, are much more simple and straightforward than the prose versions. There is only one hero, or at most two as in the *Perceval* poems, and the main interest of the story is kept clear, and not confused by side issues. Later on more characters are introduced : we follow the fortunes now of one knight now of another ; their adventures (generally with a strong family likeness to each other) cross and recross ; the titular hero disappears, often for several consecutive sections of the romance, till in the tangle the reader becomes doubtful as to which knight the compiler designed specially to honour. This tendency to diffuseness is a special characteristic of the prose romances in their later and extended form.

Another characteristic of the two sections is that in the earlier, the poetical versions, the rôle assigned to Arthur is of comparatively small importance. As M. Gaston Paris has pointed out, his court is

simply the point of arrival and departure for the
knights in quest of adventures, little or none of
the action takes place there. In the later, or
prose, romances, on the contrary, Arthur plays a
much more important part, much of the action
passes at the court, and the loves of Lancelot
and Guinevere become the central point of
interest.

It must not be concluded from the above remarks
that the romances, even the prose versons, are as a
rule wearisome to read ; on the contrary they are
charmingly written. The style is simple, direct,
and marked by a certain graceful humour which is
very attractive. I incline myself to the opinion
that the later Grail romances, the *Grand S. Graal*
and the *Queste*, with their love of far-fetched
allegory, pronounced tendency to sermonising, and
false conception of the relation between the sexes,
are decidedly the least interesting. The earlier
poets, Chrétien de Troyes, Raoul de Houdenc,
Hartmann von Aue, Wolfram von Eschenbach,
and Gottfried von Strassburg are each and all
delightful, and will well repay study.

Perhaps one might again sub-divide the versions
dealing more especially with Arthur into two
classes, the historical (or pseudo-historical) and the
romantic. That a certain historical basis for his
legend exists may be freely admitted ; how far it
extends is doubtful. *Certainly* he fought against

the Saxons, *perhaps* he was betrayed alike by his
wife and by his nephew; we can scarcely look
upon anything further in his story as based upon
fact.

The adventures ascribed to the king are not, as a
rule, of a purely chivalric character. He is a valiant
soldier and successful general; he slays monsters,
the Boar *Twrch Trwyth*, the Demon Cat of Losanne,
the Giant of Mont S. Michel, but he does not, as a
rule, rescue maidens, assail magic castles, or ride
on the Grail Quest. For adventures of this type we
must turn to the stories of the various knights, not
to those which deal with the king.

In the following pages I propose to group,
under the names of Arthur and his leading knights,
the romances dealing more directly with each;
by this means we shall succeed in classifying the
main body of Arthurian romance. Of course
certain romances will not fall under any of these
headings, as not all the Arthurian heroes immortalised in prose or verse can boast of being the
centre of a cycle; other romances, again, may
have to be mentioned more than once, as being of
importance for the study of more than one branch
of the legend; but I shall endeavour to omit no
work of solid literary or critical worth, and in the
Bibliography appended will be found full information as to the form in which each is procurable.

To begin with **King Arthur** himself, the historical basis of the whole legend is to be found in Nennius' *Historia Britonum*, compiled towards the end of the eighth century. This furnished materials for the more famous *Historia* of Geoffrey of Monmouth, written about 1136. In both of these we have an account of Arthur's struggle with the Saxon invaders, but the meagre historical element is largely intermingled with fables, *e.g.* the account of the adventures of Brutus, and the founding of the kingdom of Britain. It is to Geoffrey that we owe the introduction to the general public of the picturesque figure of the enchanter *Merlin;* a full and adequate account of the source and development of the *Merlin* legend has not yet been published. The popularity of Geoffrey's "history" was immense; it was translated into French by Wace (who added details not to be found in his source) under the title of *Li Romans de Brut*, and Wace, again, was translated into Anglo-Saxon by Layamon.

Following the same lines, but having no claim to be considered other than pure romance, is the prose *Merlin*. This gives an account of Arthur's predecessors, of his election to the kingdom, his wars with the Saxons, and early reign, carrying on the history to the birth of Lancelot. In this, its latest form, it was evidently intended to be an introduction to the prose *Lancelot*.

The first part of the romance, that dealing more

especially with **Merlin** himself, is the work of Robert de Borron, to whom other romances of the cycle are attributed; we do not know who concluded it. Two forms of the *Merlin* exist: the vulgate or ordinary *Merlin*, of which there are several MSS.; and another ending, known as the *Suite de Merlin*, which is found in one MS. alone, and of which the first four books of Malory's *Morte d'Arthur* offer an abridged translation. The "Ordinary" *Merlin* is much superior to the *Suite*, which, though it has some features of especial interest, *e.g.* it is the only authority for the fine story of Balaan and Balaain—is very diffuse and contradictory in its statements, and is, moreover, unfortunately incomplete. Both versions have been edited, and are accessible.

The latter part of Arthur's reign, and his death, are related in the French romance of *Le morte Arthur*, or *La Mort au roi Artus* (this must not be confounded with Malory's compilation, of which it forms only a small part). *Le Morte Arthur* is now generally found incorporated with the prose *Lancelot*. The *Lancelot* as a whole, though dealing more with Arthur's knights than with Arthur himself, yet contains a good deal directly relating to the monarch (*e.g.* his deception by the false Guinevere), and is, as noted above, closely connected with the "*Merlin*" in its latest and most extended form.

B

An entirely different version of the events of
the later part of Arthur's reign is presented by the
prose *Perceval li Gallois*. The author of this
romance, in common with the author of the German *Diu Krône*, was in possession of a tradition
which represented the British king in a very
unflattering light, as a slothful, self - indulgent
roi fainéant.

To sum up, the tradition of which Arthur is the
real hero is contained in the chronicles above mentioned, the *Merlin*, and the great compilation known
as the prose *Lancelot*.

One of the earliest knights connected with King
Arthur is **Sir Gawain.** He was, probably, the
centre of an independent, and it may be earlier,
cycle of adventures. He is certainly the hero of
a larger body of episodic romance than belongs to
any other knight (he is the hero of most of our
middle English Arthurian literature), and it would
be difficult to name any leading work of the cycle
in which he does not play a part, generally an
important part. At the same time he is not the
hero of any long biographical romance such as are
dedicated to Lancelot and Tristan.

The most important poems in which Sir Gawain
figures are the *Conte del Graal* or *Perceval* of
Chrétien de Troyes, and its German counterpart,
the *Parzival* of Wolfram von Eschenbach ; a good
half of these poems is devoted to Gawain, rather

than to the titular hero, Perceval. He is also
the hero of *Diu Krône* by Heinrich von dem
Türlin—a long, rambling poem with many interesting and archaic features. Here, Gawain is the
achiever of the Grail quest, in which Perceval has
failed. Gawain also plays an important rôle in
the *Chevalier de la Charrette*, and the *Chevalier au Lion*, both by Chrétien de Troyes (though
the former was completed by another hand); and
under his Welsh name of *Gwalchmei* he is a leading
figure in the *Mabinogion*, and in the fragments of
Arthurian tradition contained in the *Triad*...

A number of English metrical romances connected with this hero have been collected and
printed by Sir Frederick Madden, under the title
of *Syr Gawayne*. The chief of these, *Syr Gawayne
and the Grene Knyghte*, has more than once been
published separately.

In vol. xxx. of *Histoire Littéraire de la
France* M. Gaston Paris has given summaries of
episodic romances of which Gawain is the hero;
some of them have never been printed, some are
included in the Dutch verse translation of the
Lancelot and are found nowhere else. In the
earlier stages of the Arthurian legend Gawain is
represented as the *beau-idéal* of chivalrous valour
and courtesy, and no other knight ever gained so
firm a hold on English imagination; in our ver-
nacular metrical romances he is decidedly a more

important figure than even Arthur. He was also the "adventurous hero" *par excellence* of the cycle, and the feats ascribed to him are often of a fantastic, and even purely mythical, character. He is certainly one of the most elusive, and at the same time one of the most picturesque and charming figures of the whole legend.

Sir Perceval. Next to Gawain, the most important of the early Arthurian knights is Perceval, but his connection with the king is far less close than is the case with the first-named hero. Gawain is always and everywhere Arthur's nephew; this relationship is once attributed to Perceval (Metrical Romance of *Sir Percyvelle*), once to Lancelot (*Lanzelet*), and once to Caradoc (*Li Conte del Graal*). Save in quite the latest forms of his story, such as the *Queste*, Perceval is but a passing guest at Arthur's Court, only appearing there at long intervals; he is never an *habitué* as is Gawain.

It is generally agreed that the earliest form of his story now extant is that contained in the *Conte del Graal* or *Perceval* of Chrétien, and the *Parzival* of Wolfram von Eschenbach. The relation between these two poems has been much debated; at one time the German poem was held to be a mere translation from the French, but of late years the opinion has gained ground that the two, though ultimately going back to the same

ource, are only indirectly connected with each
other. Both are very fine poems; the French is
superior in literary style, but the German is the
more poetical in conception, and richer in human
interest and pathos. The Arthurian cycle has no
more fascinating figure than that of the lonely boy,
brought up in the wilderness by his widowed
mother, coming to Arthur's Court, an uncouth, un-
tutored lad, to demand knighthood, and gradually,
by the discipline of life, and loyal fulfilment of
natural duties, developing into a "very perfect,
gentle knight"; *A brave man, but slowly wise.*[*]
The later Perceval, the knight of the *Queste* and
prose versions, is not a very interesting figure; his
virtues are too self-conscious and proselytising; but
the early Perceval is so simple, natural, and human,
that I find it difficult to believe that his legend has
not a basis in fact.

Chrétien's *Perceval* is unfortunately extremely
difficult to obtain; but the *Parzival*, either in its
original form, in modern German, or in an English
translation, is within the reach of all. The fact
that Wagner's beautiful drama, *Parsifal*, is based
upon this poem has of late years given an addi-
tional stimulus to its study.

Perceval is also the hero of a romance by Robert
de Borron, which we only possess in a prose form;
of the Middle-English metrical romance of *Sir-*

* Wolfram von Eschenbach. Parzival. Book I. l. 108.

Perceelle of Galles; and of the prose *Perceval li
Gallois.* He is also identical with the hero of the
Welsh Mabinogi, *Peredur ap Errawc.* It is with
the legend of the Holy Grail that Perceval is most
closely connected. He is, beyond a doubt, the *original* hero of the Quest, though in the later romances,
familiar to us by Malory's translation, he plays a
rôle secondary to that of Galahad.

Into the question of the Grail romances I do
not propose to enter here; they form of themselves
an important section of Arthurian literature and
will be treated separately, and fully, by a more
skilful hand. For information on the legend of
Perceval as Grail hero the student should consult
Mr. Alfred Nutt's *Studies on the Legend of the
Holy Grail,* but from whichever point of view he
be regarded, whether as representative of a pre-
historic Aryan hero, or as achiever of the mystical
quest, he is a deeply interesting figure, and the
literature connected with him includes some of the
most fascinating romances of the cycle.

Sir Lancelot. It will, doubtless, be a surprise to
readers whose idea of the Arthurian cycle has been
founded upon Malory and Tennyson, to learn that
this knight, so important a figure in the story as
we know it, really plays a very insignificant rôle in
Arthurian literature. Apart from the great prose
compilation bearing his name (of which the adventures of other knights form no inconsiderable por-

tion), Lancelot has very little literature connected
with him. He is the hero of the *Lancelet* of Ulrich
von Zatzikhoven (which appears to contain the
earliest version of his story now extant), and of Chrétien de Troyes' *Chevalier de la Charrette.* Chrétien's
other poems barely mention his name, in the
Perceval he is not once referred to, and the only
adventure to which the most famous of Arthurian
poets alludes is that which he himself relates
in the *Charrette* poem. It seems very doubtful
whether even this adventure, the rescue of Guinevere from Meleagaunt, did not originally belong to
some other knight.

Lancelot plays a rôle in *Diu Krône*, and in a few
of the smaller episodic poems, such as *Rigomer* and
Lancelot et le cerf au pied blanc, though again in
this latter case M. Gaston Paris thinks he was not
the original hero of the tale, but the literature
connected with him is far less varied in character,
and far less important in its relation to traditional
sources, than that of which either Gawain or
Perceval is the hero.

It is to the popularity of Lancelot as the lover
of Guinevere that the commanding position occu-
pied by him in later Arthurian romance is due, and
in this character he appears first in the *Chevalier
de la Charrette.* Whether the story of the loves of
Lancelot and Guinevere is thus to be placed to the
credit of the French poet; whether it be based on

a previous legend of which some other knight was
the hero; or whether it be but a late and poor
imitation of the *Tristan* story, authorities are at
present divided. Probably the truth lies between
the last two theories. I do not myself think the
story due either to an invention or a mistake on the
part of Chrétien.

However the story arose, the fact remains that
the prose Arthurian romance in its present form
has been worked over and re-modelled in con-
formity with this, the central point of interest.
The prose *Merlin* has been extended and amplified
to serve as introduction to the *Lancelot* proper (a
process specially noticeable in the *Suite de Merlin*),
and the later Grail romances, such as the *Grand
S. Graal* and the *Queste*, if not, as seems most
probable, originally composed under the same
influence, have been submitted to a similar process
and practically incorporated with the Lancelot
legend.

As it now exists the prose *Lancelot* is a great
rambling romance, practically dividing itself into
six sections, of the first three of which, alone,
Lancelot is the undisputed hero. Of the remaining
three sections, the *Agravain* is quite as much
devoted to the deeds of other knights of the Round
Table; the *Queste* has Galahad and Perceval for its
heroes; and the *Morte d'Arthur*, though ranking
Lancelot as the first of Arthur's knights, is con-

cerned more especially with the fortune of the
King. Unfortunately this important romance has
not been edited, and is not easily accessible. M.
Paulin Paris published an abridged and modernised version of the first three sections in his
Romans de la Table Ronde (Vols. III., IV., & V.),
to which is appended an abstract of the concluding
portions. A Dutch verse translation of the last
three books exists, and has been edited by M.
Jonckbloet. It is of great value, as, judging from
the version it gives of the *Queste*, it represents an
older MS. than any we now possess; it also includes a number of minor episodic romances, some
of which are not known in any other form.

Who was the author of the *Lancelot* is uncertain,
for long popular tradition ascribed the whole vast
compilation to Walter Map and even to-day un-
critical writers are apt to make the assertion, but
students of Arthurian literature are now generally
agreed that it is extremely doubtful whether Map
ever had any hand in the matter at all. Certainly
the same author did not compose the *Lancelot* and
the *Queste*; the style of the two sections is entirely
different, and the characters ascribed to the leading
knights contradictory of each other. The *Lancelot*
and the *Morte d'Arthur* are more consistent; but
even in the earlier part of the romance we know
that one entire section, that dealing with the *Charrette* adventure, was really the work of Chrétien de

Troyes, and simply taken over bodily into the prose romance; so that the more reasonable point of view seems to be that which regards the *Lancelot* simply as a compilation drawn from various sources on which at various times many hands have worked, and for which no one writer can be held responsible. It is no more homogeneous than is the *Conte del Graal* in its extended form, and *that* is the work of at least five writers.*

Sir Tristan. It is only in the later forms of his story that this hero can be considered as in any way belonging to the circle of Arthur's knights; even then his connection with the court is, like Perceval's, intermittent, not close and continuous as in the case of Gawain and Lancelot. In the best version of the tale Arthur is but referred to as a poetical simile, and Mark is King, not merely of Cornwall, but of England also.

As a consistent and connected story, the *Tristan* legend probably took shape earlier than the Arthurian romances proper. Though it has undergone considerable development, the central *motif*, the love of Tristan for Iseult his uncle's wife, has known no change. There is no moment in the Tristan, as in the Lancelot, legend to which you can point as being anterior to the introduction of the love element.

* For the question of Map's authorship of any romance of the cycle. *cf.* Prof. Birch-Hirschfeld's *Die Sage vom Gral*, Chap. VII.

Whether the Lancelot Guinevere story be but an imitation of the Tristan Iseult legend or not, the two love tales have manifestly come into contact with and affected each other, and of the two there can be no reasonable doubt which is at once the older and the finer.

The legend of Tristan was apparently at first enshrined in detached *lais*, which, at some period not to be definitely determined, in the course of the twelfth century were woven into connected poems, probably first by *French* minstrels. These poems only exist in fragments. The most important form parts of a poem by a certain Béroul, and of one by an Anglo-Norman, Thomas of Brittany. Both were rendered into German, and these translations still exist. Béroul's version is preserved in the work of Eilhart von Oberge ; Thomas's in that of Gottfried von Strassburg. Chrétien de Troyes wrote a *Tristan* which is lost, but which some scholars incline to think lies at the root of the prose *Tristan*. This latter belongs to the same stage of Arthurian tradition as the *Lancelot* ; like it, it is a long rambling composition, differing greatly from the version of the story contained in the poems, and containing, like the *Lancelot*, a *Queste* which differs in many details from the better known *Lancelot* version.

Of all the *Tristan* romances the finest is undoubtedly the poem of Gottfried von Strassburg ; from a *literary* point of view it is probably the best romance of the entire Arthurian cycle, though *ideally* it is inferior to Wolfram's *Parzival*. In deed the German romances as a whole form a most important and interesting section of this literature ; where not direct translations from the French, a French original lies at the root of each, but in every case the German poet has treated his source with so much spirit and independence, and with so deep an insight into human nature, that the works have a character and an interest all their own. Gottfried is certainly, in grace of style, the equal even of the much vaunted Chrétien, while Wolfram is far his superior in depth of thought.

Of the *Tristan* romances the most generally popular appears to have been the prose version. Dr. Sommer remarks that it was printed more often than any other of the cycle, but unfortunately, like the *Lancelot*, it has not, so far, found an editor. Gottfried's poem, on the contrary, has been printed more than once, and can easily be obtained.

From the prose *Tristan* Malory drew largely for his compilation, which indeed represents very fairly the three great prose branches of the cycle, the *Merlin*, the *Lancelot* (including the *Queste*), and the *Tristan*. For the *Morte d'Arthur* proper, Malory seems to have used an English translation, not the French of the *Lancelot* version. Inasmuch as these prose versions represent in each case a later and complicated form of the stories with which they deal, we must not go to Malory with the idea that he will give us the original story of Arthur and his knights. The style is admirable, and the work must always remain a classic of the English language, but the picture it presents of such heroes as Gawain, Perceval, or Tristan, is very far from doing any one of them justice.

Of other knights whose names are well known, none beyond the four first mentioned possess much literary importance. Galahad, for example, only appears in the latest versions of the Grail story, the greater portion of the Arthurian literature knows nothing about him. Kay, who is certainly one of the oldest characters of the legend, probably had, at one time, romances directly connected with him. Now we only have fragmentary allusions in Welsh tradition (some of which appear to be of very ancient date) a romance *Gawain and Kay* included in the Dutch *Lancelot*, and certain poems such as *The Avowynge of Arthur* in which he plays a secondary rôle.

An important little group of poems connected with the cycle, is that of which the hero is generally termed *The Fair Unknown*; but who in the majority of instances is Guinglain or Gyngalyn, Gawain's son. These are *Sir Libeaus Desconus* (English), *Le Bel Inconnu* (French), *Wigalois* (German), and *Carduino* (Italian). Malory's seventh Book, for which no direct source has yet been discovered, probably represents a variant of this group. Inasmuch as these poems are of importance for the study of the Gawain legend, they might perhaps be classed with the literature belonging to that hero.

Of isolated Arthurian poems, we may mention *Sir Launfal*, translated and amplified from the *lai* of that name by Marie de France. Originally the story of Launfal or Lanval had, as we see from the *lai* of *Graalent* (which the English translator also used) nothing to do with Arthur; the King at whose Court the adventure takes place was anonymous, and the theme, as Dr. Schofield has shown, is a very old one. It is a good illustration of the manner in which earlier and independent stories were adapted to the requirements of an age which found its most popular theme in the Arthurian legend.

Other good examples of isolated Arthurian poems are the *Cligés* of Chrétien de Troyes, and the *Mérangis de Portlesguez* of Raoul de Houdene, but the best of this class are certainly the *Erec* and *Yvain* (*le Chevalier au Lion*) of the first-named poet. Both these works were rendered, and finely rendered, into German by Hartmann von Aue (the *Yvain* being also translated into English under the title of *Ywain and Gawain*), and of both we possess Welsh prose versions. Erec is identical with Geraint, the hero of the Mabinogi of *Geraint ap Erbyn*, while Yvain, or Owain, is

the hero of the *Lady of the Fountain* just as
Perceval is, as noted above, identical with *Peredur*.

What is the exact relationship between these
three poems of Chrétien and the three correspond-
ing *Mabinogion*, scholars have found it difficult to
decide. At one time the view was very generally
entertained that, in spite of the marked difference
of manner and matter, the Welsh stories were
only free translations from the French poems.
This was certainly an easy way of settling the
question, but there were many who felt that the
variance in matters of detail, and the very archaic
character of the Welsh tales did not lend themselves easily to such a solution. That the *origin*
of the stories is Welsh is very generally admitted.
Of late years the opinion has gained ground that
the *Mabinogion* really represent the *insular* version
as preserved among the Celts of Britain, while
Chrétien's poems represent the *Continental* version
as told by the Celts of Brittany. This seems the
truer solution and the one which accounts the best
alike for the points of contact and of divergence.
If the emigrants remembered their national
tales it seems rather absurd to suppose that their
brethren who remained in their own land should
have utterly forgotten them. At the same time,
in view of the popularity of Chrétien's fine versions (which we know, from the translation of
Yvain, came to this land), it is, of course, possible

that the final form of the Welsh stories, as we know them, has been affected by French influence.

Be that as it may, the relative part played by Celtic tradition and French genius in the formation and transmission of the Arthurian legend is a subject which will afford matter of debate for many a year to come; whether the question can ever be definitely settled is doubtful. Large as is the body of extant Arthurian literature, it is certain that it only represents a part, probably but a small part, of the original whole. Every romance that we possess postulates a previous version of the tale it tells; in no one instance would any critical scholar with a due care for his reputation venture to assert that we possess "the original story, whole and incorrupt, as it was first told."

It is not easy work to reconstruct a chain of which the primary and most important links are lacking, and those of us who undertake a share in the task must be prepared for many a disappointment. Are not the old tales parables for us? Too often we build a tower four square, and fair to look upon, only to find, like Vortigern, that there is a fatal flaw in the foundation which must needs ruin our structure. Or like the knights themselves, wandering in the enchanted forests, we find a fair-seeming road which leads us only to an impenetrable thicket, so that we must perforce retrace our steps.

But, after all, the fascination of the work itself is its own best reward, and if any one to whom this subject has been so far an unfamiliar one has a desire to try his, or her, luck on enchanted ground, it may be that these few pages will aid them in determining how and where they will begin their labours; it is only fair to warn them that they need never hope to *end* them.

CHRONOLOGICAL APPENDIX

Sixth to Eighth Century.

Building up of British heroic cycle of Arthur and his Knights. The historic Arthur died in first third of sixth century; heroic poems commemorating the struggle of Britons and German invaders were probably in existence at end of sixth or in first half of seventh century. Nennius' *History of the Britons*, in which the Arthur legend is already developed, both on the heroic and the romantic side, dates from end of eighth century.

Early Tenth Century.

Settlement of Normandy and initiation of relation between the Duchies of Normandy and Brittany, which brought the Arthur stories to the knowledge of the Normans not later than the first half of the eleventh century.

Second Third of Eleventh Century.

Norman settlements in Sicily and South Italy. Spread of Arthur legend to Italy not later than last quarter of eleventh century.

c

Second Half of Eleventh Century.

Norman conquest of England, in which Bretons take prominent part. Norman contact, partly friendly, partly hostile, with Celtic-speaking population (*a*) in South Wales, (*b*) in Strathclyde, which still retained a Cymric-speaking population.

Eleventh and Twelfth Centuries.

Considerable literary activity in Wales. Gruffyd ap Conan returns to North Wales in 1073 after stay in Ireland and holds *eisteddfodau* during his long reign, which lasted till 1137. Rhys ap Tewdur returns in 1077 to South Wales from Brittany, and may have been instrumental in uniting the two strands of Welsh and Breton romance. The *Mabinogion*, properly so-called, probably redacted in the last quarter of the eleventh century. Earlier poems, ascribed to celebrated sixth-century bards, are interpolated, added to and pastiched throughout the twelfth century. The stories of Kilhwch and Olwen, and the Dream of Rhonabwy, the only surviving Welsh Arthurian romances which antedate French influence, belong probably, in the form under which they have como down to us, to the middle of the twelfth century.

Twelfth Century.

1136. Geoffrey of Monmouth's *History of the Kings of Britain*, first draft.

About 1145. Geoffrey of Monmouth's *Life of Merlin*.

1155. Wace's French translation of Geoffrey's *History*.

About 1150-1165. Marie de France, *Lais*.

About 1150. Beroul's *Tristan*.

About 1170. Thomas' *Tristan*, professedly based on the poem of the Breton Bréri.*

---

* The *Tristan* dates are only hypothetical; the poems are so fragmentary as to yield no certain criterion of date.

1150 1182. Chrestien de Troies: *Tri tan Co*   .nt 1150, followed by *Erec*, *Cliges*, the *Chevalier de la Charrette Yvain* (between 1161 and 1173), and finally the *Conte du Graal*, written about 1182, and left unfinished by the author.

With regard to the prose Arthurian romances, it i diffi- cult to say anything more definite than that they go back substantially to the last twenty years of the twelfth cen- tury, but were continually being interpolated, added to, and reworked over until the middle of the thirteenth century, by which date they assumed the form under which they have come down to us.

First Quarter of Thirteenth Century.

Spread of the specific French Arthurian romances into Wales, giving rise to (*a*) new Welsh versions partly adapted from the French, (*b*) close and faithful Welsh translations representing earlier stages of the French romances than any existing MSS. of the latter.

BIBLIOGRAPHICAL APPENDIX

KING ARTHUR.

Nennius' *Historia Britonum*, edited by J. Stevenson for Eng. Hist. Society, about 6s.

Geoffrey of Monmouth, *Historia Britonum*, edited by Schulz 1854, about 15s. Translation of Nennius and Geoffrey in Bohn Library, 5s.

Wace, *Li Romans de Brut*, edited by Leroux de Lincy, 2 vols. 1835-38, about £1.

Layamon, *Brut*, edited by Sir Frederick Madden, 3 vols. 1847, £1 1s.

MERLIN.

Merlin (Ordinary or Vulgate), edited by Dr. Oskar Sommer, 1894, £1 16s.; *Merlin* (Suite de) from the unique (Huth) MS. edited by G. Paris and J. Ulrich, 2 vols. 1890-91, £1. A middle English translation of the *Merlin* exists, and has been edited for the Early English Text Society, 4 vols. 1865-98. *Le Morte Arthur.* Two English translations of this metrical romance exist and have been edited (*a*) by Dr. Furnivall, 1854, 7s. 6d. (*b*) for the E.E.T.S., 1865, 7s.

SIR GAWAIN.

The *Perceval* romances are classed under that heading, and *Le Chevalier de la Charrette* under *Lancelot. Diu Krône*, by Heinrich von dem Türlin, edited by Scholl, Stuttgart, 1852, about 10s. 6d.

Syr Gawayne, collection of ancient Romance poems, edited by Sir Frederick Madden, printed for the Bannatyne Club. Out of print and difficult to procure, about

C2 12s. *Syr Gawayne and the Grene Knyght*, edited ; R.
Morris for E.E.T.S., re-edited 1869 by I. Gollancz: ' , t-·
lated into English prose by Jessie L. Weston, 1-9-, 2s.
Hist. Littéraire de la France, vol. xxx. Roman, en vers
du cycle de la Table Ronde (summaries of various
romances relating to Gawain, many unedited, by M. Gaston
Paris), £1 5s. *Sir Gawain*, a study on the legend, by
Jessie L. Weston. Grimm Library, vol. vii. 1897, 4s.

SIR PERCEVAL.

Chrétien de Troyes, *Le Conte del Graal*, only printed
in Potvin's edition, 6 vols. Mons, 1866-71. Very difficult
to obtain, worth about £6 6s.

Wolfram von Eschenbach, *Parzival*, edited by Lach-
mann in complete edition of Wolfram's works, 1891, 8s. ;
edited by Bartsch (*Deutsche Classiker des Mittelalters*),
3 vols. 1875-77, 10s. 6d. This edition possesses full foot-
notes and glossaries. Several modern German translations have been published ; the most accurate is that by
Simrock (5th edition, 1863, 10s.), which is very close to
the text. San Marte's (3rd edition, 2 vols. 1887, 10s.)
translation is very free, and both Bötticher (1893, 3s.)
and Hertz cut down the "Gawain" portion, the former
omitting it altogether. Hertz's notes and appendices are
good (2nd edition, 1898, 6s. 6d.) *Parzival*. Translated
into English by Jessie L. Weston, 2 vols. 1894, 15s. net
(unabridged translation with notes and appendices). This
poem is very important for the *Gawain* legend.

Perceval, prose romance, printed by Hucher in vol. iii.
of his *St. Graal*, 3 vols. 1875-79, about £1 10s.

Perceval li Gallois, prose romance, printed in vol. i. of
Potvin's edition. A Welsh version of this exists and has
been translated by Canon R. Williams, the Hengwrt MS.,
2 vols. 1876-92, £2 2s. Under the title of *The High
History of the Holy Graal*, this romance has been trans-

lated by Dr. Sebastian Evans and published in the edition
of the "Temple Classics," 2 vols. 1898, 4s. Dr. Evans'
translation is a fine piece of work, but the inexperienced
student should be cautioned against accepting the theory
as to the date of the romance advanced in the concluding notes. It is undoubtedly a very late version of the
story.

Sir Percyvele of Galles is printed in *The Thornton
Romances*, edited by J. G. Halliwell, Camden Society,
1844. The Grail romances are fully analysed and discussed in Mr. Alfred Nutt's *Studies on the Legend of the
Holy Grail*, out of print, but so far the only *travail
d'ensemble* of the Perceval legend.

SIR LANCELOT.

Ulrich von Zatzikhoven, *Lanzelet*, edited by K. A.
Hahn. Out of print and very difficult to procure.

Roman van Lancelot, edited by Dr. Jonckbloet, 2 vols.
1850, about £1 5s. In the Introduction the editor prints
the French poem of *Le Chevalier de la Charrette*. This
Dutch Lancelot does not include the earlier part of the
history, it begins at what M. Paulin Paris calls the
Agravain section, which he considers formed the *fourth*
book of the entire *Lancelot;* but from here it is complete,
and also includes translations of several other romances,
some of which, such as *Morien*, *La Vengeance de Raguidel*,
Le Chevalier à la Manche, and *Toree* are of considerable
length and importance.

The early part of Lancelot's history is only accessible
to general readers in M. Paulin Paris' *Romans de la
Table Ronde*, 5 vols. 30s. The stories here given are
much abridged and rendered into more modern language.
A critical edition of the *Lancelot* is very much needed.

The *Chevalier de la Charrette* has just been edited by
Dr. W. Förster as vol. iv. of his great edition of Chrétien's
works, £1.

Queste del Saint Graal, edited by Dr. Furnival, 1-64, about £1 5*s.*

SIR TRISTAN.

Eilhart von Oberge, *Tristan*, edited by Grimm. 1-44. Gottfried von Strassburg, *Tristan*, edited by Bechtein, Deutsche Classiker des Mittel...), with notes and glossary, 2 vols. 1882, etc.; reprinted in a more accessible by Simrock, new ed., 1875, 9*s.*; *Tristan und Isolt*, prose translation of Gottfried's poem (abridged and modernised) by Jessie L. Weston, 2 vols. 1899, 6*s.* The fragments extant of Thomas of Brittany's *Tristan* were edited by Michel, but the book is out of print. A new edition is being prepared by M. Ernest Muret.

Le Roman en Prose de Tristan, critically analysed by E. Löseth, 1892, 15*s.* This gives a summary of the contents of the prose romance, with the principal variants. In default of a modern edition of the *Tristan* this book is most valuable. *Der heutige Stand der Tristan Forschung*, Dr. W. Röttiger, gives a summary of the present state of investigation into this interesting legend.

———·———

Sir Thomas Malory, *La Morte d'Arthur*. The best edition is that by Dr. O. Sommer, 3 vols. 4to, 1889-91 £2 10*s.*, which exactly reproduces the original text. Vol. iii. (*Studies on the Sources of Malory*) is of special value to the student of Arthurian romance in general.

The Avowynge of Arthur, edited by Robson for the Camden Society (*Three Early English Metrical Romances*), 1842, 4*s.*

MINOR CYCLES.

Sir Libeaus Desconus. Several times edited ; latest edition by Kaluza, 1890, 10s.

Renaut de Beaujeu, *Le Bel Inconnu*, edited by Hippeau. A full summary is given in *Hist. Litt.* xxx.

Wirnt von Gravenburg, *Wigalois*, edited by Pfeiffer, 1847. Out of print.

A. Pucci. *Carduino*, edited by Rajna, 1873.

The above four poems, their relation to each other and to the *Erec* of Chrétien de Troyes, have been fully discussed by Dr. Schofield : *Studies on the Libeaus Desconus.* Harvard Studies, vol. iv. 1895.

Sir Launfal, printed by Ritson, *Ancient English Metrical Romances*, 1802.

Marie de France, *Lais*, edited by Warncke, 1885, 10s.

Raoul de Houdenc, *Méraugis de Portlesguez*, edited by Friedwangen, 1897, 10s.

Chrétien de Troyes, *Cligés*, edited by W. Förster, 1889, 4s. *Yvain (Le Chevalier au Lion)*, edited by W. Förster, 1891, 4s. ; *Erec*, edited by W. Förster, new and corrected edition, 1896, 6s.

Hartmann von Aue, *Iwein* (*Deutsche Classiker des Mittelalters*), edited by Bech, 1888, 7s. ; *Erec* (*Deutsche Classiker des Mittelalters*), 1893, 6s.

Yvain and Gawain, edited by Schleich, 1887. 6s.

Mabinogion, edited by Lady Charlotte Guest, 1877, 18s.

A comparative study of the relation between the French and English Yvain and the Welsh Mabinogi will be found in the *Modern Quarterly for Language and Literature*, Nos. 2 and 3 (July and November 1898).

.

Printed by BALLANTYNE, HANSON & Co.
London & Edinburgh

www.ingramcontent.com/pod-product-compliance
Lightning Source LLC
Chambersburg PA
CBHW021442090426
42739CB00009B/1608